Transitioning to Swift

A Guide for Objective-C Developers

Table of Contents

1. Introduction 1

2. Understanding the Basics of Swift 2

   2.1. Why Swift? 2

   2.2. Syntax Primer 2

   2.3. Variables and Constants 3

   2.4. Data Types and Optionals 3

   2.5. Control Flow 3

   2.6. Functions 4

   2.7. Classes and Structures 4

   2.8. Concurrency in Swift 5

3. Decoding Objective-C: A Refresher 6

   3.1. The Heritage: Smalltalk 6

   3.2. The Syntax: Square Brackets and Messages 6

   3.3. The Types and Type Safety: Dynamic vs Static Typing 7

   3.4. Foundation and Cocoa: Essential Frameworks 8

   3.5. Objective-C Runtime 8

   3.6. Memory Handling: ARC and Manual Retain-Release 9

4. Distinguishing Between Objective-C and Swift 11

   4.1. Similarities 11

   4.2. Syntax 11

   4.3. Memory Management 12

   4.4. Type Safety and Inference 12

   4.5. Optionals 12

   4.6. Error Handling 13

   4.7. Strings 13

   4.8. Speed 13

   4.9. Protocols and Extensions 13

5. Setting up Your Swift Development Environment 15

5.1. The Swift Programming Language … 15

5.2. Understanding Xcode … 15

5.3. Installing Command Line Tools … 16

5.4. Configuring Xcode for Swift Development … 16

5.5. Swift Syntax Highlighting and Indentation … 16

5.6. Running Your First Swift Program … 17

5.7. Utilizing Playgrounds for Swift … 17

5.8. Setting Up Version Control … 17

5.9. Debugging in Xcode … 18

6. Swift Syntax: A Comprehensive Overview … 19

6.1. Variables and Constants … 19

6.2. Collections … 19

6.3. Control Flow … 20

6.4. Function Syntax … 21

6.5. Swift Optionals … 21

6.6. Conclusion … 22

7. Swift for Objective-C Developers: A Detailed Comparison … 23

7.1. The Fundamental Differences … 23

7.2. Understanding Basic Structures … 24

7.3. Control Flow and Looping Structures … 26

7.4. Functions and Methods … 27

8. Effective Transition Strategies: From Objective-C to Swift … 29

8.1. Understanding the Similarities and Differences … 29

8.2. Embracing the New … 29

8.3. Getting Familiar with Swift Syntax … 30

8.4. Planning for Effective Transition … 31

8.5. Leveraging Apple's Interoperability … 31

8.6. Understanding Common Pitfalls … 31

9. Dealing with Common Challenges in Swift for Objective-C Developers … 33

9.1. Understanding Swift Syntax 33

9.2. Memory Management 34

9.3. Working with Optionals 35

9.4. Swift Error Handling 36

9.5. Protocol-Oriented Programming 36

10. Capitalizing on Swift's Advantages: Advanced Features and
Techniques 39

10.1. Embracing the Safety and Speed of Swift 39

10.2. Functional Programming in Swift 40

10.3. Swift's Optionals 41

10.4. Error Handling in Swift 41

10.5. Protocol-Oriented Programming 42

11. Case Studies: Real-world Transitions from Objective-C to Swift . 44

11.1. Journey of AppXYZ: An E-commerce App 44

11.2. Rewrite of GameDEF: A Popular Gaming App 45

11.3. Transformation of AppGHI: A Social Media Analytics Tool . 45

11.4. Conclusion 46

Chapter 1. Introduction

In the rapidly evolving world of coding, keeping abreast of changes is vital. Our Special Report, "Transitioning to Swift: A Guide for Objective-C Developers" serves as an indispensable manual for those looking to navigate this shift seamlessly. The technological realm may appear complex, yet this guide demystifies the process of shifting from Objective-C to Swift. We've distilled the essence of this technical adaptation into easily comprehensible terms, encouraging developers at all levels to embark on this journey of learning. There's no fluff, no jargon - just tried and proven strategies that will propel you forward in your programming career. Get ready to unfurl the new programming vistas and unravel the mystery of Swift with access to this informative guide.

Chapter 2. Understanding the Basics of Swift

Swift, Apple's powerful and intuitive programming language, offers a robust set of features for developers, especially for those transitioning from Objective-C. It is known for its efficiency and powerful capabilities, which serve as the backbone of popular apps and technologies.

2.1. Why Swift?

The language is relatively straightforward and less verbose than Objective-C, offering clarity without compromising expressiveness. Its robust typing system and error handling can minimize and simplify code, providing savings in maintenance and debugging time.

Swift also includes advanced features like generics, closures, tuples, and optionals, which not only enrich the language but also help streamline and improve your code performance.

2.2. Syntax Primer

Swift syntax is clear and intuitive. The rules are simpler and less ambiguous, meaning you spend less time fixing syntactical errors. The "Hello, World!" program, arguably the simplest program to write in any language, can be implemented in Swift using this one line of code:

```
print("Hello, World!")
```

2.3. Variables and Constants

Swift differentiates between variables and constants. Variables can represent a value that can be changed over time, defined via the `var` keyword. On the other hand, constants hold a value that remains unchanged throughout the execution of a program, defined using the `let` keyword.

```swift
var myVariable = 42
myVariable = 50
let myConstant = 42
```

In the aforementioned code, `myVariable` is variable, with its value changing from 42 to 50, while `myConstant` is a constant, and its value of 42 remains unchanged throughout.

2.4. Data Types and Optionals

Swift is a strongly-typed language, meaning you must explicitly define the types of all your variables. Swift supports all standard types, such as `Int` for integers, `Double` and `Float` for floating-point numbers, `Bool` for Boolean values, and `String` for textual data.

Optionals represent a variable that might hold a value or might be `nil`, and are a safe and expressive way to structure your code.

```swift
var optionalInteger: Int?
```

2.5. Control Flow

Swift control flow statements, including `for-in`, `if-else`, and `switch`, are similar to other C-family languages you may be familiar with.

```swift
let individualScores = [75, 43, 103, 87, 12]
var teamScore = 0

for score in individualScores {
    if score > 50 {
        teamScore += 3
    } else {
        teamScore += 1
    }
}
```

2.6. Functions

In Swift, functions are first-class types, so they can be nested, passed
around as a variable, and returned from another function. To define
a function, use the `func` keyword, followed by the function's name, a
parameter list, and the return type.

```swift
func greet(person: String, day: String) -> String {
    return "Hello \(person), today is \(day)."
}
```

2.7. Classes and Structures

Swift supports object-oriented programming with classes and
structures. Classes are reference types, while structures are value
types.

```swift
class Shape {
    var numberOfSides = 0
    func simpleDescription() -> String {
        return "A shape with \(numberOfSides) sides."
```

```swift
    }
}

struct Square {
    var sideLength: Double
    func area() -> Double {
        return sideLength * sideLength
    }
}
```

2.8. Concurrency in Swift

Swift provides several approaches for concurrent programming. Grand Central Dispatch (GCD) and NSOperationQueue are some of the most commonly used mechanisms, enhanced by Swift's ability to run closures concurrently.

Through this exploration of Swift's basic elements, you have garnered vital tools for constructing your Swift programs. Remember, the secret to mastering Swift is practice and hands-on experience. Happy coding!

Chapter 3. Decoding Objective-C: A Refresher

Before embarking on the adventurous journey of transitioning to Swift, we need to revisit the foundational principles of Objective-C. This chapter will refresh your memory about Objective-C's semantics, syntax, and other basic elements.

3.1. The Heritage: Smalltalk

Objective-C has its roots in the Smalltalk programming language, designed in the 1970s. It is an object-oriented language that allows multiple inheritance and has a dynamic typing feature. The influence of Smalltalk can be seen in the way objects are created, methods are invoked, and messages are passed in Objective-C.

Consider this line of code from Smalltalk:

```
myObject doSomethingWith: this and: that
```

It clearly lays out the object (`myObject`), the method (`doSomethingWith:and:`), and the parameters (`this`, `that`), bringing out an intuitive human-like sentence structure that is easy to read and understand. This philosophy manifests into the deftness of Objective-C.

3.2. The Syntax: Square Brackets and Messages

The dynamic and intuitive nature of Objective-C owes to its syntax. Let's look closer:

```
int result = [myCalculator add:5 toNumber:3];
```

In the given example, `myCalculator` is the object, `add:toNumber:` is the selector and $(5,3)$ are the parameters. The method call resides inside the square brackets, returning an integer, 'result'. The selector acts as a bridge between the object and the method. If this was written in Swift, the syntax would look like: `var result = myCalculator.add(5, toNumber: 3)`

Understanding the syntax is pivotal in transitioning from Objective-C to Swift. Swift has a more compact and less verbose syntax which is one of the reasons developers are transitioning to it.

3.3. The Types and Type Safety: Dynamic vs Static Typing

Objective-C, owing to its Smalltalk heritage, is dynamically-typed. Unlike C++, Java, or Swift, Objective-C doesn't emphasize type safety. It allows for greater flexibility, but at the expense of potential runtime errors that a statically-typed language like Swift could catch at compile time.

Here is an example of dynamic typing in Objective-C:

```
id myObject;
myObject = @"A string";
myObject = @(42);
```

We declared an object `myObject` of type `id` which can hold any type of object. Then we assign it a string and a number without any compiling problems. However, this can lead to unexpected runtime issues if not handled carefully. Swift, on the other hand, strongly adheres to type safety and requires explicit type declarations, unless the type can be inferred.

3.4. Foundation and Cocoa: Essential Frameworks

Cocoa is the application framework for Mac OS X, and Foundation is part of Cocoa. They contain the classes, data types, and functions familiar to Objective-C developers. Whether it's working with strings, arrays or dates, these frameworks work as the backbone for any Objective-C programmer. An understanding of these platforms is essential for a seamless transition to Swift, particularly since Swift has equivalents for these classes (though some bear different names).

Objective-C:

```
NSString *name = @"John Doe";
```

Swift:

```
var name = "John Doe"
```

In Swift, creating a mutable string is as swift as creating an immutable string while, in Objective-C, NSMutableString is used for creating mutable strings.

3.5. Objective-C Runtime

The Objective-C runtime is what makes Objective-C truly unique. It's a library located in the core of the operating system that enables all the basic features of Objective-C, such as dynamic typing, dynamic binding, and dynamic loading. Through the runtime library, Objective-C objects can interact, perform operations, create classes, and generate new methods during the execution of the program.

For instance, consider this line of code for dynamic method creation:

```
objc_allocateClassPair(MyClass, "MySubclass", 0);
```

In Swift, the runtime is part of the language, but it's less explicit and somewhat hidden. Swift's features like protocols, extensions, optional chaining, etc., are provided by the Swift runtime library, which is incorporated into your apps when they're built.

3.6. Memory Handling: ARC and Manual Retain-Release

Objective-C once relied entirely on manual memory management. Developers were required to allocate and deallocate memory, increase and decrease object reference counts, and prevent memory leaks and orphan objects. The introduction of ARC (Automatic Reference Counting) simplified this process significantly. Even so, understanding memory management is still advantageous, especially when transitioning to Swift.

Consider the following example which wouldn't cause a compiler error in Objective-C, but could cause memory retention:

```
property (retain) id delegate;
```

In this case, Swift's automatic and sophisticated memory management system prevents such problems. Swift employs ARC, like Objective-C, but extends it with a feature called Automatic Reference Cycles to avoid cyclic dependencies and memory leaks.

While Objective-C and Swift share many commonalities, the

differences are significant. Leveraging your understanding of Objective-C will aid in the transition to Swift, giving you a strong start on the path to mastering this powerful language. Our next chapter will delve into the world of Swift, further preparing you for your journey. Remember, the beauty of Swift lies in its simplicity and conciseness coupled with powerful features like optionals, generics, and closures. So, let's dive in!

Chapter 4. Distinguishing Between Objective-C and Swift

Despite their coexistence and aim to execute largely identical tasks, Objective-C and Swift display marked differences. Having a comprehensive understanding of these distinctions lays a solid foundation for transitioning from the former to the latter.

4.1. Similarities

To alleviate the fear of treading into an utterly foreign territory, it's essential to first consider the shared traits between Objective-C and Swift. As Apple's software development tools, both languages facilitate the creation of powerful applications and excellent user experiences. Moreover, they both allow the interfacing with Apple hardware capabilities and access to a broad range of APIs that permit interaction with system components and services. They also present themselves in the popular Integrated Development Environment (IDE) Xcode. These overlapping features should provide Objective-C developers some comfort.

4.2. Syntax

On the surface, and perhaps the most glaring difference between the two languages is syntax. As an extension of the C programming language, Objective-C adheres to much of C's syntax, including the use of semicolons (;) to end lines and braces ({}) to group blocks of code. On the other hand, Swift drops these requirements. The absence of semicolons makes Swift syntax cleaner and more streamlined as it only uses braces for grouping.

Another notable distinction is the usage of square brackets in Objective-C. Procedures are typically invoked within these notations, which is not the case in Swift. Swift uses the more conventional dot notation for method invocation, which many may find more intuitive.

4.3. Memory Management

A substantial change in Swift, albeit mostly hidden to the programmer, is its approach towards memory management. Objective-C uses a system called Automatic Reference Counting (ARC) to manage memory. While Swift also utilizes ARC, it introduces an additional concept of optionals and forced unwrapping, which aids in avoiding null reference exceptions, a common headache in Objective-C development.

4.4. Type Safety and Inference

Swift places more emphasis on type safety than Objective-C. It enforces variable types more strictly at compile-time, which can reduce runtime errors. Additionally, Swift introduces type inference. The language is shrewd enough to understand what type a particular variable is, negating the need to explicitly declare the type in many circumstances.

4.5. Optionals

Swift introduces to iOS developers a fantastic new feature: the Optional Type. A variable of optional type either contains a value or is null. This is unlike Objective-C, where the absence of a value is represented by a separate 'nil' or 'NULL' object. The optionals in Swift add a layer of safety, mitigating the infamous "null pointer exceptions".

4.6. Error Handling

Both languages contain error handling, although their approaches differ quite a bit. Objective-C uses a system of try and catch blocks alongside NSError objects passed by reference. On the other hand, Swift provides easy-to-use constructs including 'throw', 'try', and 'catch', similar to many modern languages. This approach is more comforting to developers from non-Objective-C backgrounds.

4.7. Strings

Objective-C treats strings as objects of the class NSString (or NSMutableString), whereas Swift treats them as structures. This leads to a more intuitive syntax for string, making Swift more intelligible for beginners.

4.8. Speed

Swift was explicitly created to be faster than Objective-C. And indeed, in many respects, it does perform more efficiently. That said, your actual mileage may vary depending on the specifics of your code and how you use the language.

4.9. Protocols and Extensions

Both Objective-C and Swift use protocols to define behavior. However, Swift takes this a step further with protocol extensions, where common behavior can be defined for classes that conform to the protocol.

These are just a few of the many differences between the two languages. Each developer's transition may present unique challenges and advantages, but understanding these fundamental contrasts can armor you with the knowledge needed to dive headfirst into the world of Swift programming.

Next, we will delve into the specifics of Swift, like declaring variables, creating arrays or dictionnaries, handling control flow, error handling, writing and calling functions, and using classes and structures. To master Swift, understanding these basics is vital. Rest assured that following chapters will elaborate on these concepts in depth. Prepare to immerse yourself into the vast ocean of Swift programming.

Chapter 5. Setting up Your Swift Development Environment

Getting your Swift Development Environment set up is the first crucial step towards transitioning from Objective-C to Swift. More than just downloading the right software and tweaking a few settings, it is about understanding the tools you would be working with and why you are using them.

5.1. The Swift Programming Language

Swift is a powerful, fast and intuitive mixed-paradigm language developed by Apple for iOS, macOS, watchOS, and tvOS app development. With its concise yet expressive syntax and modern features, Swift offers developers a rich and interactive coding experience. Often heralded as the future of iOS development, understanding Swift is a necessity for modern developers.

5.2. Understanding Xcode

Xcode, Apple's Integrated Development Environment (IDE) is the central tool when developing in Swift. It comes with a robust set of features that not only assist in writing and debugging code, but also provide interface builders, testing engines, and asset workflows.

To install Xcode, navigate to the Mac App Store, search for Xcode, and click on 'Get'. Once installed, it's a good practice to check the version using the terminal. Type `xcdode-select --version` and hit enter.

5.3. Installing Command Line Tools

Although Xcode is a hefty platform that includes the command line tools necessary for development, it is prudent to ensure these tools have been installed separately as well. In terminal, enter `xcode-select --install`. A prompt will appear for you to download the command line developer tools.

5.4. Configuring Xcode for Swift Development

Having installed Xcode, it is time to get acquainted with your new development environment. Open Xcode and create a new project. Select 'Single View Application' and name your application. Under 'Language', select Swift.

It might be worth noting that Xcode projects start with a set of default files. Main.storyboard is where you will design your app, AppDelegate.swift and ViewController.swift are Swift files, and Info.plist contains various settings.

5.5. Swift Syntax Highlighting and Indentation

Xcode comes with syntax highlighting for Swift. You can customize the colors by clicking Xcode → Preferences → Fonts and Colors. There is also an automatic indentation feature which can be customized under Text Editing.

5.6. Running Your First Swift Program

Writing your first program is as simple as opening the ViewController.swift file in Xcode, locating the `viewDidLoad()` function, and writing the following print statement inside it:

```
print("Hello, Swift!")
```

Now, hit the 'Run' button at the top or use the `cmd + R` shortcut to launch the app on a simulator. If everything has been set up correctly, "Hello, Swift!" will appear in your debug area at the bottom of the screen.

5.7. Utilizing Playgrounds for Swift

One of the most impactful features of Xcode is Playgrounds. This is a space where you can experiment with Swift code and see the results without the need to build and run an app. To launch, select File → New → Playground, name your playground, and select 'Blank' for the template.

5.8. Setting Up Version Control

Version Control System (VCS) is crucial for maintaining different versions of your codebase and reverting changes if needed. Available directly within Xcode, you can set it up during the initial creating process of your project or through Xcode → Preferences → Source Control.

5.9. Debugging in Xcode

The built-in LLVM compiler within Xcode comes with a debugger suite that can be used to optimize your Swift code. Learn to set breakpoints, inspect variables, and control the execution flow using this essential tool.

This setup of your Swift Development Environment is just the first step toward building complex and efficient applications using Swift. Although there may seem to be a lot to understand and adapt to initially, with time and practice, these tools will play an instrumental role in enhancing your Swift development proficiency. Let this journey towards Swift not be one of apprehension but one of exploration and learning. Happy Coding!

Chapter 6. Swift Syntax: A Comprehensive Overview

Swift is a statistically typed language that uses the LLVM compiler, inherited from Objective-C. This allows for improved type-checking at compile time, eliminating many common programming errors. Swift defines away common programming faults by altering how you code. In this chapter we are going to dive deeply into Swift syntax and take a tour of its many features.

6.1. Variables and Constants

In Swift, you define your variables using the 'var' keyword and constants using the 'let' keyword. Swift also allows you to infer the type of variable or constant, which can be found very useful for cleaner code. Below is an example that introduces variables and constants:

```
var variableName = "Hello, Swift"
let constantName = "Hello, Swift"
```

Please notice, Swift is strictly type safe. Once you've set the type for your constant or variable you cannot change it. Trying to assign a value of a different type will lead to a compile-time error.

6.2. Collections

Swift provides two kinds of collections: arrays and dictionaries. Array is an ordered collection whereas dictionary stores unordered items. Here's how you define an array or dictionary in Swift:

```
var someArray = [Int]()
var someDictionary = [String: Int]()
```

In the above code, 'someArray' is an empty integer array and 'someDictionary' is an empty dictionary whose keys are strings and values are integer types.

6.3. Control Flow

In Swift, control flow statements (loops and conditional statements) are similar to other C-family languages with some refinements inspired from other languages.

For instance, a basic 'for' loop:

```
for i in 1...5 {
    print(i)
}
```

In the above example, '...' represents the inclusive range from 1 to 5.

An example of 'if' statement:

```
let temperature = 30
if temperature <= 20 {
    print("Cold")
} else if temperature <= 30 {
    print("Warm")
} else {
    print("Hot")
}
```

6.4. Function Syntax

Functions in Swift are defined with the 'func' keyword. Here's how you can declare a function in Swift:

```swift
func functionName(parameterName: parameterType) ->
returnType {
    // Code
}
```

An example of a function that adds two integers:

```swift
func addTwoIntegers(a:Int, b:Int) -> Int {
    return a + b
}
```

Functions can also have multiple return values, which can be very useful in complex algorithms and data manipulations.

6.5. Swift Optionals

Optionals are a Swift feature that deals with the absence of a value. The concept of optionals doesn't exist in C or Objective-C. The nearest thing in Objective-C is the ability to return 'nil' from a method that would otherwise return an object.

Optional in Swift is represented using '?' symbol. Here's a simple example:

```swift
var optionalString : String?
```

In this example, 'optionalString' has no value by default. We need to provide a value before accessing it, otherwise, it'll lead to a runtime crash.

6.6. Conclusion

In conclusion, Swift has a powerful and intuitive syntax that designers have refined by learning from other modern languages. It's simple and expressive, which ultimately makes the entire process of programming easier and more fun.

By adding type inference, optionals, and several other features, Swift has not only improved upon Objective-C in many ways but also introduced a whole new syntax that can be easy to understand for developers coming from various different languages.

Swift is interesting, fast, modern, safe - and this chapter has provided a comprehensive overview of its syntax. You've learned about how variables and constants, collections, control flow, functions and even optionals work in Swift. This knowledge forms the foundation on which you'll be able to build more complex Swift applications. Now that you have a solid understanding of Swift syntax, the next step in your transition to Swift will be to explore the functionalities and design patterns that Swift has to offer.

Chapter 7. Swift for Objective-C Developers: A Detailed Comparison

Understanding the transition from Objective-C to Swift begins with noting the key differences and similarities between the two. Let's break down the distinct aspects of Objective-C and Swift, shedding light on how you can comfortably transition from one to the other.

7.1. The Fundamental Differences

Swift and Objective-C may have a lot in common, but they also have fundamental differences that shape the way each language is programmed.

1. Syntax In Objective-C, the syntax is a concatenation of the Smalltalk and C programming languages. As such, it can be quite verbose and convoluted for some developers. On the other hand, Swift favors a more simplified and concise syntax that is easier to read and write.

For example, let's consider a simple hello world program:

In Objective-C:

```objc
#import <Foundation/Foundation.h>

int main(int argc, const char * argv[]) {
    @autoreleasepool {
        NSLog(@"Hello, World!");
    }
    return 0;
```

```
    }
```

In Swift:

```
print("Hello, World!")
```

As evident, Swift requires significantly fewer lines of codes and is more simple and straightforward.

1. Safety Swift's syntax and language constructs exclude certain types of mistakes possible in Objective-C. For instance, Swift will produce a compile-time error when you write a code that could potentially lead to a null reference exception.

2. Speed Swift also provides various speed advantages during development, such as faster algorithms for sorting and searching.

Now that we have an overview of the major defining differences, let's delve into the specifics of coding.

7.2. Understanding Basic Structures

Both programming languages share a common ancestry in C. Understanding the differences in basic structures will provide a solid foundation and enable a seamless transition.

1. Variables In Objective-C, you need to define the variable data type specifically. Swift, conversely, uses type inference.

Objective-C:

```
NSString *string = @"Hello, world!";
```

Swift:

```
var string = "Hello, world!"
```

1. Constants Objective-C uses the `const` keyword, whereas Swift uses `let` to define a constant.

Objective-C:

```
const int number = 10;
```

Swift:

```
let number = 10
```

1. Arrays and Dictionaries In Swift, arrays and dictionaries are typed, and the syntax is more straightforward.

Objective-C:

```
NSArray *array = @[@"item1", @"item2", @"item3"];
NSDictionary *dict = @{@"key1" : @"item1", @"key2" : @"item2"};
```

Swift:

```
var array = ["item1", "item2", "item3"]
var dict = ["key1": "item1", "key2": "item2"]
```

7.3. Control Flow and Looping Structures

Control flow and looping structures are indispensable components of any programming language. Let's observe the difference in Swift and Objective-C.

1. if Statements Just like in Objective-C, Swift uses the if statement to execute code based on a certain condition. However, Swift's if statement does not require parentheses.

Objective-C:

```objectivec
int number = 10;
if (number > 5) {
    NSLog(@"Number is greater than 5");
}
```

Swift:

```swift
var number = 10
if number > 5 {
    print("Number is greater than 5")
}
```

1. For Loops Objective-C supports both traditional and enhanced for loops. Swift, on the other hand, supports a range of loop structures.

Objective-C:

```objectivec
for (int i = 0; i < 10; i++) {
    NSLog(@"%d", i);
```

```
    }
```

Swift:

```
for i in 0..<10 {
    print(i)
}
```

Swift, however, offers for-in loop, which is an easier way to iterate through an array.

```
for item in array {
    print(item)
}
```

The critical part to remember here is the simplicity and readability of Swift compared to Objective-C. The shift in syntax promotes cleaner code, fewer bugs, and overall, an easier transition.

7.4. Functions and Methods

Objective-C and Swift treat functions and methods slightly differently. In Swift, functions are a first-class object, which means they can be nested and even passed around in variables.

1. Defining Functions Defining a function in Swift requires the `func` keyword.

Objective-C:

```
- (NSInteger)addNumbers:(NSInteger)number1
withNumber2:(NSInteger)number2 {
```

```objc
    return number1 + number2;
}
```

Swift:

```swift
func addNumbers(number1: Int, number2: Int) -> Int {
    return number1 + number2
}
```

1. Calling Methods In Swift, you call a method by providing its name
   and any arguments it accepts.

Objective-C:

```objc
NSInteger result = [self addNumbers:5 withNumber2:3];
```

Swift:

```swift
var result = addNumbers(number1: 5, number2: 3)
```

The transition from Objective-C to Swift involves a learning curve,
but once the basics are understood well, the scope of transition
amplifies, leading to a polished understanding of the newer platform.

By fortifying your understanding of these critical components,
shifting from Objective-C to Swift becomes a structured,
straightforward task. It allows you to write safer, more reliable code,
opening up a world of opportunities in iOS and MacOS development.
Now is the best time to make this transition - the future of iOS and
MacOS programming lies with Swift.

Chapter 8. Effective Transition Strategies: From Objective-C to Swift

To effectively transition from Objective-C to Swift, it's crucial to understand the similarities and differences between these languages, the new offerings of Swift, and the strategies related to the conversion process. Let's dive in.

8.1. Understanding the Similarities and Differences

Despite the intrigue prompted by Swift's novel offerings, Objective-C is still very much in the loop. Stemming from C, Objective-C is a superset of that language, incorporating object-oriented capabilities and a dynamic runtime. Swift, on the other hand, albeit having roots in C and Objective-C, is more syntactically concise and embraces a safer programming pattern.

Recognizing these differences and similarities aids in transitioning as it sets clear expectations about what to encounter. However, it's equally important to not hastily discard your knowledge of Objective-C. Both languages can coincide in your codebase and Apple has place structures to ensure compatibility.

8.2. Embracing the New

Swift has ample features that set it apart from Objective-C:

- Swift is more modern, safer, faster, and enables a level of interactivity in development.

- It has a clean and expressive syntax which makes the code more readable.

- It is easier to maintain since it does not have separate interface (.h) and implementation files (.m).

- Swift does not expose pointers and other unsafe accessors.

- It has strong typing and optionals, which makes Swift code more predictable.

Grasping these new elements is vital in acclimatizing to Swift. They represent Swift's leaps from the C and Objective-C lineage, and understanding them can put you in good stead for the way ahead.

8.3. Getting Familiar with Swift Syntax

Swift's syntax is concise and less cluttered. Below are some syntax comparisons:

Objective-C:

```
NSString *someString = @"Hello, World!";
```

Swift:

```
let someString = "Hello, World!"
```

As visible, Swift syntax is succinct and embraces a 'less code' philosophy. Spend time familiarizing yourself with these changes and practice writing them.

8.4. Planning for Effective Transition

Transitioning languages does not necessitate an abrupt phasing out on ongoing projects. A progressive phased rollout is recommended to minimize disruptions.

1. Start by writing unit tests in Swift: It's a good place to start using the language where it will not affect the application's main functionality.

2. Then, develop new features with Swift: This allows you to gradually increase the amount of Swift codebase.

3. Gradually rewrite old parts: As you gain confidence, start rewriting old Objective-C code parts in Swift during any code changes or bug fixes.

8.5. Leveraging Apple's Interoperability

Apple's interoperability allows Objective-C and Swift code to live side by side in the same project, sharing the runtime, which makes the transition process less disruptive. It ensures that the old, Objective-C code will not be obsolete suddenly and it can be rewritten gradually. So you can make a steady shift without disregarding Objective-C entirely.

8.6. Understanding Common Pitfalls

Like any transition, moving from Objective-C to Swift comes with common pitfalls. Most commonly, developers may struggle with:

1. Swift's optionals and error handling: Swift's way of dealing with nullability and errors is different and initially might be

confusing.

2. Memory management in Swift: ARC works slightly different in Swift including the way the weak references are handled.

3. The shift from dynamism to static: Swift moves away from the dynamic nature of Objective-C which leads to a different style of coding.

Equipping yourself with the knowledge of these pitfalls and their respective remedies will ensure a smoother transition.

Certainly, adapting to a new language involves time and effort. This guide is intended to pave your path with more clarity, forming a systematic approach to the shift. Embrace Swift and its powerful features, keeping in mind that it's not a replacement but an advancement. There's plenty of room for Objective-C and Swift in your toolbelt, and knowing both will only serve to amplify your abilities!

Chapter 9. Dealing with Common Challenges in Swift for Objective-C Developers

While migrating from Objective-C to Swift, developers are likely to encounter several common challenges. Successfully addressing these can make the transition smoother and more efficient. We'll cover these dilemmas and provide strategies for overcoming them in the sections ahead.

9.1. Understanding Swift Syntax

Swift's syntax is a drastic departure from that of Objective-C. However, it's intuitive and designed with clarity in mind. It involves fewer @ symbols and more English-like statements.

Let's look at defining a class:

Objective-C:

```
@interface MyClass : NSObject
@end
```

Swift:

```
class MyClass: NSObject {
}
```

There are no @interface/@end or @implementation symbols, and Swift uses colons to specify class inheritance, much like other C languages. Swift classes, unlike Objective-C objects, can be instances of their own type.

It will take practice to acclimate to Swift's concise, human-readable syntax. Starting with small conversion projects will help.

9.2. Memory Management

Swift uses Automatic Reference Counting (ARC), similar to Objective-C, but it's more stringent about memory leaks related to circular references.

Consider the following:

```swift
class MyClassA {
    var b: MyClassB?
    deinit {
        print("A is being deinitialized")
    }
}

class MyClassB {
    var a: MyClassA?
    deinit {
        print("B is being deinitialized")
    }
}

var a: MyClassA? = MyClassA()
var b: MyClassB? = MyClassB()

a?.b = b
b?.a = a

a = nil // Will not call deinit
b = nil // Will not call deinit
```

Here, you will not see the "A is being deinitialized" and "B is being deinitialized" prints, indicating a memory leak. Swift solves such issues using weak and unowned references.

9.3. Working with Optionals

An incredible safety feature Swift provides is the concept of Optionals. An Optional is a type that can hold either a value or no value (nil). This is disparate from Objective-C, where nil is often used interchangeably with zero, false, or an empty state.

Consider an instance where we try to access a non-existent dictionary value:

Swift:

```swift
let dict = ["foo": 1]
let notExists: Int = dict["bar"] // This will give an
error
```

Here, `dict["bar"]` is an optional that may contain an Int. It has to be unwrapped before used, indicating that you are acknowledging this could be nil. For example:

```swift
if let value = dict["bar"] {
    print(value)
}
```

It's vital to adapt to using Optionals properly to avoid runtime errors in Swift.

9.4. Swift Error Handling

One clear departure from Objective-C is Swift's error handling model. Swift uses a separate language construct (`throws`, `do`, `try`, `catch`) for errors that can be thrown and caught. This is a significant leap over the NSError out parameters in Objective-C.

A sample function that can throw errors in Swift might look like this:

```swift
func canThrowErrors() throws -> String

do {
    let result = try canThrowErrors()
} catch {
    print(error)
}
```

Meanwhile, an equivalent Objective-C function might look like this:

```objc
NSError *anyError;
NSString *result = [self
canThrowErrorsAndReturnError:&anyError];
if (anyError) {
    NSLog(@"%@", anyError);
}
```

Swift's error handling is more expressive and safer, preventing unforeseen runtime errors.

9.5. Protocol-Oriented Programming

Swift is not just an Object-Oriented language; it's also a Protocol-Oriented language. This means Swift's protocols allow developers to write more flexible and reusable code.

Consider a scenario where Classes A, B, and C need to share some common behavior. In Objective-C, you would likely specify this behavior in a superclass and then make your A, B, and C classes subclasses of this superclass.

In Swift, by contrast, you would create a protocol specifying this common behavior. Classes A, B, and C can then be types that conform to this protocol.

Let's see this in code:

Objective-C:

```objc
@interface MySuperclass : NSObject
- (void)doSomething;
@end

@interface MyClassA : MySuperclass
@end

@interface MyClassB : MySuperclass
@end

@interface MyClassC : MySuperclass
@end
```

Swift:

```swift
protocol DoSomething {
    func doSomething()
}

class MyClassA: DoSomething {
```

```swift
    func doSomething() {
    }
}

class MyClassB: DoSomething {
    func doSomething() {
    }
}

class MyClassC: DoSomething {
    func doSomething() {
    }
}
```

Switching to this new paradigm of Protocol-Oriented Programming can have profound implications in the way that you architect your applications.

In this chapter, we touched upon some challenges that Objective-C developers might encounter when transitioning to Swift. This includes syntax differences, stricter memory management techniques, optionals, error handling, and protocol-oriented programming. However, once you overcome these challenges, you'll find that Swift is a powerful, expressive, and rewarding language to work with.

Chapter 10. Capitalizing on Swift's Advantages: Advanced Features and Techniques

Starting any task is less daunting when one is familiar with the available tools and how to apply them. In this context, Swift's robust advantages and advanced features are your toolkit. By familiarizing oneself with these unique features and techniques deployed by Swift, Objective-C developers can expedite their transition journey. The tips and techniques encapsulated in this chapter are designed to help you fully harness the power of Swift.

10.1. Embracing the Safety and Speed of Swift

First and foremost, Swift provides a significant advantage in both safety and speed over Objective-C. Thanks to its robust typing system and error handling, programming nightmares such as null pointer dereferencing are a thing of the past.

Adding to this, the language itself has been fine-tuned for performance. It can outpace Objective-C in several computing scenarios, which means that it not only makes your code safer but also faster.

Swift's modern, expressive syntax makes your code cleaner and less error-prone. With Swift, there is no need for semicolons at the end of each statement, and braces are no longer required for conditional statements. As a result, your code will look cleaner, be easier to read, and contain fewer errors.

Let's look at how Swift syntax differs from Objective-C:

```swift
let sampleString: String = "Hello, Swift"
let sampleArray: Array<String> = ["Apple", "Banana",
"Cherry"]
let sampleNumber: Int = 10
```

In the above example, we declare a string, an array, and an integer. As you can see, the syntax is straightforward, easy to understand, and less cluttered than the Objective-C equivalent.

10.2. Functional Programming in Swift

Secondly, Swift incorporates many principles from functional programming languages. This includes first-class and higher-order functions, which can lead to cleaner, more modular code.

Higher-order functions are an integral part of Swift and introduce powerful ways to manipulate data. Swift provides the functions 'map', 'filter', and 'reduce' that can be applied directly on collections, such as arrays and dictionaries.

For instance, let's filter an array of numbers to obtain only the even ones:

```swift
let numbers = [1, 2, 3, 4, 5, 6]
let evenNumbers = numbers.filter { $0 % 2 == 0 }
```

The resulting array, 'evenNumbers', will consist of the even numbers in the original 'numbers' array ([2, 4, 6]).

10.3. Swift's Optionals

Swift's optionals indicate that a variable might hold a value or might hold no value at all (nil). While other languages have nullable types, Swift's optionals come with a powerful suite of operations that make it easy to handle these "maybe" values.

Hence, Swift's optionals provide a safe way to deal with the absence of a value. They reduce errors caused by trying to access a nil value, which implicitly contributes to code safety.

Consider a dictionary lookup:

```
let nameDictionary = ["John": 32, "Anna": 28, "Steve":
40]
let johnsAge = nameDictionary["John"]
```

In the above example, if "John" exists in the dictionary, `johnsAge` will be an optional with the value 32. If "John" does not exist in the dictionary, `johnsAge` will be nil.

10.4. Error Handling in Swift

Swift has built-in support for throwing, catching, propagating, and manipulating recoverable errors at runtime. It uses a syntax that is consistent with the rest of the language, providing a clear and expressive way to handle errors as opposed to relying on error-returning codes and exceptions.

It provides developers with the `do-catch` statement to handle errors explicitly. Consider the following fictive example:

```
do {
    try someThrowingFunction()
```

```
    }
catch error {
    // Handle Error
}
```

In the above block, the `try` keyword is used before a function that can throw an error. If an error occurs within the `do` block, it is propagated and handled within the `catch` block.

10.5. Protocol-Oriented Programming

Beyond traditional object-oriented programming, Swift emphasizes the use of protocol-oriented programming (POP). POP encourages us to develop flexible, decoupled, and reusable code through protocols.

In Swift, using protocols, protocol inheritance, and protocol extensions, we can create highly adaptable code, opening the door to unlimited possibilities of code design and organization.

```
protocol Drawable {
    func draw()
}

class Circle: Drawable {
    func draw() {
        // Implements drawing functionality for Circle
    }
}

class Rectangle: Drawable {
    func draw() {
        // Implements drawing functionality for Rectangle
    }
```

```
    }
```

In the above example, the `Drawable` protocol defines a method called `draw`. Any class or structure that adopts this protocol needs to provide an implementation for this method.

Getting comfortable with these Swift features lays a solid foundation for your transition from Objective-C. However, it's important to note that the key to mastering Swift is regular practice. The deeper you delve into Swift, the more you'll notice how these features interconnect to provide a seamless and efficient coding experience. Your journey may be challenging, but the rewards that Swift has to offer make it an adventure worth embarking on.

Chapter 11. Case Studies: Real-world Transitions from Objective-C to Swift

The transition from Objective-C to Swift can appear to be a daunting task, primarily due to the profound differences in syntaxes and paradigms employed by the two languages. However, upon closer examination and introspection, developers have often found that Swift provides a significantly more streamlined, efficient, and functional programming experience. In this context, several case studies of real-world transitions lend valuable insights to those contemplating the transition.

11.1. Journey of AppXYZ: An E-commerce App

AppXYZ, an established e-commerce mobile application, was written entirely in Objective-C. The app had hundreds of thousands of lines of code distributed across multiple modules. However, prolonged build times and a codebase that was complex and less safe raised concerns.

The transition came, phase-wise. The team decided to write new modules in Swift, while older modules were gradually rewritten and tested. One of the challenges the team faced during the conversion process was the interoperability issue when Objective-C and Swift were used in the same project. This was addressed using the Objective-C Bridging Header, which allowed Objective-C classes to be accessed in Swift.

By the time of completion, the codebase was reduced by approximately 30%, and the readability was enhanced due to Swift's expressive syntax.

11.2. Rewrite of GameDEF: A Popular Gaming App

GameDEF, a popular Gaming app, had a user base of over 1 million. Written completely in Objective-C, the initial feedback from users indicated performance bottleneck issues which arose from lack of optimization. Swift's more advanced functionalities, and the promise of better performance, made the transition appealing.

It all started with creating a Swift project and rewriting the performance-critical modules. GCD (Grand Central Dispatch), a low-level API available in Swift, was used to optimize multi-threaded code and ensure smoother gameplay. Transitioning was not a smooth ride, due to the significant differences between the two languages, especially around memory management, and optionals handling.

Though the process faced its challenges, GameDEF's performance improved post-transition. Additionally, decreased complexity and increased safety made debugging easier, thus reducing maintenance time and costs.

11.3. Transformation of AppGHI: A Social Media Analytics Tool

The application, AppGHI, was a social media analytics tool that had a relatively older codebase written in Objective-C. The factor motivating the transition was the scarcity of Objective-C developers, sluggish modernization updates, and the significant shift towards Swift in the iOS community.

The transition strategy in this case prioritized the app's components critical for business logic and higher user interactions. By strategically selecting features to be converted, AppGHI developers managed to distribute the conversion effort logically and efficiently.

Towards completion, the application moved away from MVC (Model-View-Controller), which is more prevalent in Objective-C, to MVVM (Model-View-ViewModel), a design pattern which harmonizes better with Swift's features, thereby enhancing readability and maintainability.

Not only did the switch lead to a more modernized tool, it also brought about reduction in overall project size. The transition proved beneficial in attracting more iOS developers due to the prevalence of Swift in developer communities.

11.4. Conclusion

Each of these real-world examples, while unique on their own terms, share a common thread. That being, the transition to Swift, while challenging, leads to a more streamlined development process, simplifies maintenance, and offers inherent performance optimizations. Strategically planned and executed transition practices enable Objective-C developers to adapt to the ever-evolving iOS programming landscape and keep their applications up-to-date with modern iOS development practices, swiftly and efficiently. The keys to a successful transition include a well-thought-out strategy, stepwise adaptation, and continued learning in the process. In the end, the rewards surpass the effort, making Swift a highly appealing choice for iOS development.